WHAT BOOKS PRESS

AN IMPRINT OF

THE GLASS TABLE

COLLECTIVE

LOS ANGELES

OTHER COUNTRIES

POEMS

RAMÓN GARCÍA

For JQ, our own
Jenny on the block.
I'm glad to have
gotten to know you,
thanks for all
the work you do —
and for being
fun.

Sincerely,

Ramón

10-21-2010

WHAT
BOOKS
PRESS

LOS ANGELES

Grateful acknowledgment is made to the to the editors of the following journals in which these poems, or earlier versions of them, appeared. "Whitman in the Suburbs" and "Sodom and Gomorrah" appeared in *Chaparral*. "Summer" appeared in *The Flight of the Eagle: Poetry on the U.S.-Mexico Border*. "Acapulco, 1965" appeared in *The Paterson Review*. "El Jalisco" appeared in *Ambit*. "Hansel in the Jungle" appeared in *Mandorla: New Writing From the Americas*.

A very special thanks to the colegas in the Glass Table collective, my colleagues at CSUN, my family in Modesto and my adopted family in downtown Los Angeles. The writing of these poems has been supported by residencies at the MacDowell colony, the Virgina Center for the Creative Arts, and the Ragdale Foundation. I have benefited from participation in Cecilia Woloch's Paris Poetry Workshop and workshops at the John Ruskin Art Club in Los Angeles led by David St. John and Molly Bendall. I owe much to the insight and generosity of Helena María Viramontes, Terry Wolverton, Marisela Norte, Maria Elena Gaitan, Patssi Valdez, Gregory Mertl, Gronk, Ricky Ridecos, Richard Mcdowell, Caroline Le Duc, Ondine C. Chavoya, Rita Gonzalez, Roberto Tejada, Terese Svoboda, Saskia Hamilton, Jeff Allen, Mikhail Iossel, Camille Norton, Elena Karina Byrne, Sergio de la Mora, Anna Sandoval, Ricky Rodriguez, Sandra de la Loza, Sirena Pellarolo, Trebor Healy, Adolfo Guzman-Lopez, Juan Felipe Herrera, Manuel Muñoz, Harry Gamboa Jr., Francisco X. Alarcón, Lorna Dee Cervantes, Ruben Mendoza, and Luis Vega.

Publisher's Cataloging-In-Publication Data

Garcia, Ramon.
    Other countries : poems / Ramón García.

    p. ; cm.

Poems in this book, or earlier versions of them, appeared previously in various journals.
ISBN-13: 978-0-9823542-6-1
ISBN-10: 0-9823542-6-6

1. Mexican Americans--California--Poetry. 2. California--Poetry. 3. American poetry--Mexican American authors. I. Title.

PS3607.A73 O85 2010
811./6   2010928213

What Books Press
23371 Mulholland Drive, no. 118
Los Angeles, CA 91364

WHATBOOKSPRESS.COM

Cover art: Gronk, *Fallen Tower*, mono print, 2010
Book design by Ashlee Goodwin, Fleuron Press.
Author photo: Matthew Alvarez

OTHER COUNTRIES

for Matthew Alvarez

CONTENTS

¡Sigue tranquilamente! ¡Oh caminante!,
todavía te queda muy distante
ese país incógnito que sueñas...

Rubén Darío

I The Son

VALLEY NEWS

Out in the fields bordering the suburbs
an eighteen year old Oaxacan girl, six months pregnant,
collapsed picking grapes in the 110 degree heat.

Nonetheless, the summer has resurrected
itself on air conditioning, Kool-Aid,
Little League baseball games, swimming pools...

I have already lived this summer
and will have to live it once again.

I wonder what happened to those
poor white prostitutes with bad teeth
who worked the sad motels on Crows Landing Road
and their junky brothers
riding bicycles wearing someone else's
ripped blue jeans
all the days of all the summer afternoons
of my American childhood
the pawn shops in Modesto are still circulating
their stolen knives and watches.

The Mexicans keep coming into the Valley
they will keep coming as long as there are summers
and crops and the manufactured fruits of the earth.

Oh, Lord, the kids will be playing baseball,
the swimming pools will be boiling,
by the Fourth of July there will be a murder or two
in the Airport district, where gangs are fighting.
There is no way to leave the summer.

GRAY LANDSCAPE

I drive through the flat suburban roads of Modesto.
Gray asphalt suppresses all colors
below the red-tinged skies of sunset:

I am no one, I've done nothing,
and suddenly I know nothing.
The world outside the Valley does not exist—

And the times and places that have been mine—
a rainy afternoon in Teotihuacán,
one uncanny evening overlooking
the mountains of Lorca's Granada,
the many sunsets mirrored in Echo Park lake,
the Coalcomán nights of my childhood,
downtown L.A. beneath the tentative light of dawn—
lie dormant, withdrawn,
for again,
I am inside the monotonous labyrinth of Modesto,
the gray annihilation of the suburbs as the sun sets.

GOLDEN HIGHWAY

Bisected by the 99 Highway, this town,
A city really, from which a cowtown
Has not managed to extricate itself.

The trees, the grape vines, the fruit,
Mexican hands tend, grow, gather them,
But idylls come to an end here,
In the fields and the factories.

And these are the ranches of the Portuguese,
Of the Italians who did well,
Ranches that don't look like ranches,
That are tract homes at the margins of
Orchards, with four wheelers in driveways
And basketball hoops, for years
Used by kids who went to the city,
Or moved two miles into town.

And here are the fields again
Landlocking the suburbs.
And the vineyards the Valley is known for.
Farms—so many—and cows too,
Inside the pastured assembly line corrals,
Crowded together, heavy with the patient
Storing of slaughter. They stink up the air.

From car windows city faces look out and
See another town as the 99 rolls on.

In another hour and a half, San Jose,
In two hours, the San Francisco bay.
The wealth of a nation festers here.
The cows are well-fed, the ranches
Spawn another ranching generation.
The Mexicans work, burned by a familiar sun,
They live as in Mexico still, most of them,
This is their children's land.

THE PRODIGAL SON COMES HOME

They rejoice without noticing
I sleepwalk in memories
Of cities, music, sex, drunkenness.

I am back where I ended
    Amid innocence and injustice.

No more will I see the sun rise over polluted oceans
Paris in dreams of gold as the sun dies
The madhouse of Los Angeles' downtown
The moody lights of the nightclubs and the headlights
Of traffic at night, the splendor of foreign faces
And the lips of strangers offering themselves
          Forever or for one night.

There is peace in the fields, silence in the
House. Work to be done, love to give back.
My life was lived away from here.

ACAPULCO 1965

Here is Mom, wearing a one-piece bathing suit
and Dad next to her
with his arm around her shoulder,
looking like they never will again—
she with Dolores Del Rio hair
and he with the Elvis Presley pompadour and dark sunglasses.
It is their *luna de miel*, Acapulco 1965, and they are
on the beach, smiling, the ocean in black and white behind them.
Is Mom a virgin still or is this the day after?
Do they love each other? And how?
What are they thinking? What dreams do they share?
They do not know of trailers in Modesto, the feel of peach fuzz on the skin
and the hot fields, flat and heavy across Central Valley afternoons.
The fruit-picking and the canneries would come later,
after Dad continues his card-playing
and his father sends him and his new wife *al norte*.
They are as I've never
seen them or imagined them to be.
Did they kiss back then?
Did they like each other's company? Were they content?
In that other country? In that other life?
And what of the losses and the gains?
Of the Mexican children who never turned out as planned?

THE OTHER COUNTRY

We ordered books, posters, notebooks
from catalogues the teacher gave us:

Once, I bought with my allowance
a reproduction of a painting
of a dead Indian collapsed upon
a horse's back, an arrow piercing
his spine. Behind the Indian's bent
back, dark mountains rose, a sunset
blazed as if pumped up with blood.

I taped the poster to the bedroom wall.
My brother's posters of KISS
and mine, of Blondie,
gave it a serious, school-like air,

the only image my brother and I shared.
The picture of the Indian hung
on the wall of my classroom
that year, an icon of nobility in America.

A war had just ended
many more were to come.

We lived in History

In pop music and tragedy.
It was all adapting to us.

SUMMER

The sun grips the suburbs
through the air conditioned hours.

Time weighs suspended
when Mom is working
the afternoon shift at the cannery.

Dad has come home from work
and is asleep on the couch.

The television is on, sounding unwatched images.
There are bicycles that have been ridden to exhaustion
       baseball games long ended,
the smell of peeled mangos and peaches,
      disco songs on the radio.

Life was awful in a wondrous way
in the unnamable misery of childhood
      that knows no sorrow—
      and stays forever in place.

THEME

In the land of fairy tales
every boy is a brother,
all girls are little mothers,
in other words, sisters.

Every city is a forest
where we cannot make a home.

Mirrors are storehouses of beauty and hate.

Animals talk, reminding us of relatives.

Every kiss recalls a prince, a witch,
an old man, a cold-hearted mother.

HANSEL IN THE JUNGLE

We have walked alien paths
Trying to find our way back to what we know.

Liver-colored parrots with the faces of old perverts
Steal the bread we dropped to map a return.
Starved into savagery, they descend
To eat the traces of our escape.

The sky's gluttonous dimness expends itself.
Massing, bourgeoning shadows rush above us
Through the cavernous heights of the trees.

Inhuman echoes, then the scarce ravenous light,
The oppressive odor of leaves warmed by the furtive sun.

We hear the greedy gurgling of water,
Nervous whisperings from nearby streams,
The hungry green world turning,
Turning on its cruel machinery.

Lightening cracks beyond the canopy
Of intertwined branches.
A scream rings from the bowels of the jungle.
"It's a monkey," Gretel says.
But it sounds like fear itself.

Before us, murky trails pave
Into our history—that German obscurity.

The night will come to shut us in,
Our sad hunger will feed
The inescapable famine of evil.

GENERATIONS

At Grace Lutheran Elementary School
the kindergarteners participate in
     a graduation ceremony;
their sporty midget cheers ring out
     like those of college grads
from the front pews of the church.

First grade is a whole summer ahead of them,
     summer is a huge span of life.

My niece Natalie, the graduate,
chooses the Red Robin restaurant
in Riverbank for her graduation lunch
she loves the runny macaroni and cheese
     and the French Fries.
After lunch we visit the fish, turtles and snakes
     at the Pet Barn pet shop.

In Riverbank the beige dreams
of four-car garage tract houses
have spread over the land,
the peach fields keep shrinking.

Riverbank is where the so-called Brown Buffalo
the legendary Chicano writer came from
     where if you saw the lonely
cows that are still grazing
     in the remaining farms,
     the gray canneries
and the town's picturesque water tower,
you would understand why all of it

in a time of segregation and Chuck Berry
        could drive a man crazy.

You would understand what would lead
Oscar Zeta Acosta to disappear off the coast
        of Mexico
        or go insane—
he did both, but then he was an excessive man.

I know there are infinite varieties
        of saying no to geography.
There are colorful prodigal son wanderings,
not a bad option that includes exotic locales,
and a back up plan in case all else fails.
There are the numerous existential poses
requiring study and application of book lessons
that in the end are not truly applicable,
and worst of all, out of fashion! Yet, worthwhile,
because they can serve as a rite of passage.
So many choices, indeed, available to sons
        of the San Joaquin Valley
who decide to make a life elsewhere.

And yet there is no way to leave the silence that
        descends over the Valley at night
on the locked mini-malls fronted by blocks
        of empty parking lots
lit up with lights meant for no one.

The prisoners inside the jail on J Street
        downtown know the valley is a prison
and that one prison
        is as good as any other.

HOLIDAY INN

I'm a bus boy at the Vineyard Restaurant at the Holiday Inn
The summer after high school graduation.
I pick up greasy dishes, wipe tables, and take food up to the rooms.
I wear a uniform: black polyester slacks, long sleeve white shirt, black bowtie,
Black vest, and polished black dress shoes.
I'm skinny, brown and shy.

Tourists pass through Modesto on the way to Yosemite or San Francisco.
They spend the night and check out the next day.
They don't leave the hotel. There are businessmen from Cincinnati,
French farmers come to learn the ways of growing peaches in the Valley.
One time, an actor from Stark Trek dines alone, and orders a bottle of wine.

The waiters and waitresses see me as an outsider.
I won't be working at the Vineyard Restaurant the rest of my life.
Maybe that's why Ida, the head waitress, isn't nice.
Ida, who keeps my tips, is Chinese and tough, she
Has a daughter and no husband; smokes like a survivor.
She's worked at the Vineyard restaurant for decades.
So has Mr. Duran, a Mexican who has kids my age.
He gossips about Daniel, the cook, a big burly guy—
He's gay, some of his friends are dying of AIDS.

The manager and his wife come to the restaurant now and then.
The manager's wife is a bitch. Condescending, haughty,
She inspects the silverware, scrutinizes the food on her plate.
I get nervous serving her the Chicken Piccata.
She always finds something to complain about:
The silverware is not polished to her liking

And Ida says it's because I never make sure
The knives and forks are clean.

Saturday nights there's live music in the restaurant's bar.
The musicians are a married couple, friends of the manager and his wife.
They sing Elvis songs and Beatles tunes.
After the show, like old friends, they all get drunk.

One time, I get a call to deliver hamburgers to one of the rooms.
It's some old ladies having a party.
Ida looks me over accusingly, suspicious.
I take the tray stacked with hamburgers in round plastic containers
To the suite of the partying seniors.
One lady asks my name, says they're having a birthday celebration.
She tells me to smell the perfume on her neck.
"What do you think," she asks in a breathy voice.
"It's nice," I say. She pats my cheek, eyeing me flirtatiously,
Then hands me a ten dollar tip.

Another time a man orders room service dinner.
Ten minutes later he wants another coke.
When I return to the room, a single Coke on my plastic delivery tray,
He opens the door wearing a white towel around his waist
As if he had just stepped out of the shower, but he isn't wet.
He's older, maybe thirty, and has the hairiest chest I've ever seen.
He's rich, his face is not the face of white people in Modesto.
He darts his eyes around the room looking for his wallet,
Tells me to sit down, smiles, reads the name tag
On my chest, "You have an elegant name," he says,
"What do you do for fun?"
"Hang out with friends, go to the movies," I say.
I'm nervous. I'm scared to look at him.
He gives me a twenty dollar tip and tells me that I'm very nice.
"What time do you finish work?" "Ten o'clock," I stammer.
"Feel free to come bye and say hello before you leave," he says.

I'm not the only one who gets propositioned.
Cindy, the new hostess, does too.
She's come from a cold state with lots of snow.
She's past thirty and completely alone.
Like Ida, she steals my tips.
After work the businessmen in town for some convention
Wait for her in the parking lot that burns black and lurid the whole day
Next to the 99 Freeway.
Petite Cindy climbs into a Bronco with them—they're all white, tall and
Athletic—
She pretends not to see me as I step inside my car.
"She's a slut," Mr. Duran tells me the next day. "No one will ever marry her."

After I pick up all the trays that have been left
Outside of rooms I've made deliveries to
I punch my time card and leave by 10:30,
I go home to read the *Diary of Anaïs Nin*.
Anaïs Nin is in Paris with Artaud and everyone's in love with her.
I know I'll never lead a fascinating life.
I want the summer to end.
I want college to begin.
I don't know who I am.

HORSES

From the top of the bunk bed
I shared with my brother,
we watched the news on television.
        Boats packed with skinny Cuban refugees
rocked on scary waters towards Florida shores.
        We couldn't speak about the sadness.

        I was in the 5th grade, and liked disco music.
I knew all I was supposed to know.
When I took my citizenship test five years later,
        I confused Cuba with Puerto Rico
                and failed.

"They're a bunch of criminals, communists and homosexuals,"
Mrs. Carpenter lectured. "President Carter is a moron.
We should let the sharks eat them..."

        A dictator of common sense
with short hair and plain flat shoes
        Mrs. Carpenter kept framed photos of her horses on her desk,
they had weird white girl names: Brandi, Stella, Minnie...
        She lived out in the country,
but in Modesto it was hard to tell where the suburbs ended
        and the country began.

Mrs. Carpenter had been my brother's teacher too.
She was an earthy lady
and didn't mean so much harm.
I know it, but I don't understand—
this sadness, my brother, we became.

INHERITANCE

After the metropolises and small towns
The rural trains and undergrounds
I'm back in this flat scene—
The suburbs as existential stage set.

What was the role I left behind
But never managed to abandon
With death the one and only understudy?
Even the plants and hedges propped
About the overly related houses
And the sunflowers in the alleys
Have taken direction from the city planers.

The actors become their roles:
        A family dialogue.
I unspool the script—entangled in
The spirit and knotted in the flesh—
That was transcribed by mute experience
In the alien language of a true self.

The lights are bothersome
And the audience is tired.
Three Acts: a minor epic entitled
        Family Life.

PETS AND TEACHERS

It was a squat school
Painted a muddy orange
That dulled the morning light.

At Orville Wright Elementary School
Classes lost the school district's spellathons
The academic decathlon,
Little league baseball teams never
Made it to playoffs.

Once, there was a rabid possum
On the monkey bars
It's enraged red eyes and vampire teeth
Claiming the sandbox.
Animal control people in protective gear
Took it away,
But its ratty demon face

Is still there, in the pacified days
Of childhood, in the school playground
Where the kids tormented Melanie,
The dimwitted girl.
It was terrible, the name calling,
The cruel games, and yet I only remember
Her sandy hair,
That standing in line behind her
Waiting to reenter the classroom after recess
She smelled like rancid maple syrup.
I was one of the guilty,

But I could never live with the guilt.
Later it became part of how I lived,
Or did not live.

      And the boy with the chopped-off hand?
It was said his father had done it.
One of the boys batted for him
At baseball games during lunch hour;
He was a good catcher with his other hand
And he and I took turns playing center field.

Sometimes I suspect I never left those
Mornings at Orville Wright reading the letters
Of the American alphabet lining
The top of the chalkboard above me,
Like the stations of the cross during mass
Or those afternoons memorizing the lessons
Of my parents' fatigue after the fields or the canneries
While the television droned away the summer hours
With laugh tracks.

      And into this melancholy tableau
Of the West, let me introduce Mrs. Hicks,
Who screened documentaries about endangered seals.
When I was in college, I went to look for Mrs. Hicks.
I was told she had moved to Las Vegas.
And what I would like to know is this—
Did she ever know love?
Did anyone hold her and make her scream
With pleasure as I imagine every woman
Made for this world should be?
Was she a gambler, a lesbian?
Did she read Dostoevsky or set foot
On foreign soil?

She knew the poor whites neglected
Their pets, and she assumed that because
The Mexican parents loved and protected
Their children so much
Their animals were accorded
The same family affections.
She would ask about our dog, Chief.
I knew not to tell her that when the family
Went to Mexico for Christmas
The pit bull disappeared. It was a willed
Carelessness that made Chief leave.
And so Mrs. Hicks would be
Disappointed to know
That she was wrong about us
As it was better that we knew

So little about the disappointed world
Of adults, since we were
Being prepared for it in our games
And in our loneliness
In what would never make sense,
And live forever through us.

THE SUMMER OF *JAWS*

It was the summer of *Jaws*.
The beach loomed to a spooky soundtrack
      on the screen at the McHenry Cinema.

      A real shark came to the Valley that summer.
In the 115 degree heat of the Montgomery Ward's parking lot,
      a huge trailer with a life size shark
painted on the entirety of its sides
      lured viewers to a real life *Jaws*,
the big screen's shark doppelgänger inside.

      Tia Lisa took my brother and me to see
the shark on a scorching afternoon.
      She was the most Americanized of the *tias*,
the most permissive, she had let us watch
      Saturday Night Fever.

The great terrible creature inside the freezing trailer,
          was a marvel
      its jaws opened for us to gape into,
with teeth as real as the fish stench:
      a cold dead dream
visiting the stagnant enchantment of our childhood.

MANUEL

I knew him when his beauty
was all of a piece:
        his high cheeckbones,
        the empty radiance
        of his good looks,
        the impeccable smile
of a Mexican boy from Modesto.

I last saw him entering a Goodwill store.
Out of curiosity, I followed him in.
Carrying a soiled backpack
        he talked to himself.
The girl at the cash register
        made a sour face.
        Was he homeless?
It was not age that marred his face—
madness ravaged him, drugs and
self-betrayal. He was not all there.

Once he had danced under
        eternal disco lights,
glamour dizzying around him with
enviable promises. Nothing was real.
Nothing is real still, but the beauty
is gone, and the music and the sparkling
lights. I didn't want him to recognize me.
I ran out, into the suburban streets
        we both had come from.

THE LOVE OF CHILDREN

I. Gretel's Confession

Neglected, abused, sold off,
we came upon our destiny—
and gave ourselves to the deepest candies,
sweet surrogate motherings.

We were becoming the witch's children.

But then we had to kill her
and share her death
the strongest bond we've ever known.
Not even love can come between it,

nothing will ever separate us.

II. Hansel's Defense

The witch filled mother's absence with gluttony.
Her huge loneliness offered to limitlessly feed us,
and we didn't know when to stop.
Greedy Gretel, gorging on the delicacies of ugliness
wanted more.

The flames, bristling with the witch's screams
lit traces of mother on Gretel's delicate face.

How can she be so beautiful?
I see myself in her and know that I must leave her.

DEPARTURES

You will leave many cities

They will all be different
Until you hand over your absence
To them

Every leaving
Hankers after your childhood
Mapping the Modesto suburbs
Into all the distances

You will love many cities

But the cities will continue
To leave you

THE OCEAN, HOME

In a California of migration, baseball games and
Peach orchards, I never thought about
The ocean, humming eternally its great depths
A few hours away, or the Sierras, even closer,

Or the redwoods. An inland childhood—the plainness
And heat of the San Joaquin Valley in the summer,
The chill of the suburbs in winter could do
Without the memory of a sea, seen as a child,

In Manzanillo, and the volcano in Colima, which had
Fascinated, once...In adolescence, I saw San Francisco
With Mom and her friend Rafaela, who also
Worked summers at the cannery.

We visited offices where Mom signed
Papers for her green card. And in a restaurant
Somewhere in the city, in voices full of pity
The women in my life said San Francisco was

A modern day Sodom and Gomorrah. There was smog
Coming in from the gray city distances. And sadness
Everywhere, in the high rises and the hills,
On streets where the sinful walked.

I never thought to live there.
One summer, years later, I did.
You have to try to understand a sort of innocence
That's dangerous: I was in love and I thought

It would last forever. I tasted the sexual salt
In the cold breeze of the bay, and I knew
What all prodigal sons know:
That isolation prepared me for exile.

That parents age in the silent, unchanged
Countries that they abandon and make us inherit.
That the lights of all cities are
Lotus flowers. That even loneliness sings

Irresistible songs in unshared beds in apartments
We will never own. That we never had a choice
About coming home, which is why we never will.

II Prodigal Cities

GREYHOUND STATIONS

Terminals, way stations
where congressed teenage runaways,
hustlers from backwater towns,
defeated prodigal sons,
trysting lovers rich in adultery
        but penniless.
Where is she now? The battered woman
hiding a black eye behind scratched sunglasses,
holding an imitation leather suitcase patched up
with duck tape, her lacquered face
a sister to the mask worn by the drag queen
standing by the gumball machine, who was escaping Texas
with a one way ticket to New York, Las Vegas or Hollywood.
        And the immigrant families
traveling across state lines with their broods of kids,
Diego Rivera's Indian children, but in sneakers
and jeans, their Mervyn's clothes sticky with ice cream
Chirping, chirping, in English, in Spanish . . .

        For years the discarded buses
languished in neglected parking lots
and now their itineraries are erased.

SODOM AND GOMORRAH

The palm trees are more beautiful
For being fake.

Winter harbors banished doses of sunlight
And when the rare rains come, like a distraction,
The earth laps up the downpours,
The residents dance in a wet frenzy.

Though the sunlight is piercing, luminous
Its people prefer the unlettered neon lights
Out of which deception mounts and spirals
To extinction
In the insatiable lightlessness of the sky.

In the ephemeral papers, in the immortal books
When the city burns
They call it God's judgment,
Reckoning and fulfillment.

But those who live here
Incessantly paying high taxes to the flesh
Know it as belonging—
The construction of monuments of pleasure
From the architecture of ashes and lust.

SKYSCRAPERS

Insomniac brightness inside empty offices
and cubicles black with lightlessness.

A checkered pattern of illuminated
and blackened squares climbs
the Library Tower's height.

Numinous night. Unequal buildings.
Sleep. The temporary absence of crowds,
the hibernation of work and its forces.

INNER CITY

In that famous photograph
Lorca wears a black bowtie
His eyes glimmer intensely
like the eyes of gypsies or saints.

In Spain, so many decades back,
A crime ended those eyes, but not
The nocturnal light they harbored,
Or dreams and death, Lorca's Geminis...

The cholos let out of jail,
They wander the L.A. streets downtown,
And have the poet's eyes too. If you
Catch their furtive glances,
You can see the light of
Days lost to deranged angels,
Beautiful, tragic angels of history,
The kind that would have appealed to
The Andalusian poet. And in the
Eyes of these gangsters is the stabbing
Darkness of the city night, sketchy with
Stray lights escaped from the high rises
When the masses are locked in by banal dreams.

Though Lorca sleeps forever in Granada
His myths flower in the detritus of the metropolis:
Duendes play surrealist games
At the Hollywood Wax Museum
And design the outfits for
The Santos Niños de Atocha
At the Boyle Heights Mercado.
The lemon trees in the backyard
Of a campesino from Sinaloa in
Lincoln Heights scent the air with
Memories, with Mexico and Death.

LOS ANGELES

Art Deco buildings in ruin
Downtown is a simulacrum of Mexico City
Inflamed phosphorescent sunsets
The view of the Hollywood sign
When driving up Highland Avenue

Skyscrapers, gingerbread bungalows
Labyrinths of floating freeways

Echo Park Lake a mirror
To city lights, moon-solarized palms
A sky morphed with the skyline

Driving on Sunset Boulevard
Traffic lights and stray sounds
Flashback and fast cut repetitions of
Motel neon signs, ghettos, lust,
Hovering moons, memories of deserts
Traversed by residues of the tropics

In this city
Which is all cities and all dreams
A presentiment of death.

PALM SPRINGS

Night lights, parched glittering sands,
Luxury, retirement, death.

The encircling mountains, bland mounds of time,
Are picturesque and immense, silent as memory.

They come here for soul cures, for orgies, for the unobstructed stars
That feed arid hungers born in other cities, other towns.

A land for television actors, retired movie stars
Insipid city of the plain made for the thousands

Who know pleasure, their last hours and final fears here
In a landscape as pure and destroyed as biblical salt.

The sugar daddies eye shop with desperately exquisite glances
Gleaming of money, comfort and slavery.

For the poor it is barren and indiffrent,
A paradise for bimbos, native ground for rattlesnakes and coyotes.

A city that won't stop being a desert
Under a sky that won't relinquish its ancientness,
Expensively blue and blank, like a newly bought heaven.

RETURNING TO LOS ANGELES AFTER THREE WEEKS IN RUSSIA

The palms are a brotherhood
of flags propped up on the landscape.

The 105 freeway runs through a
nexus of overpasses, above ground.

The sprawling grids of suburbs
without pattern or boundaries.

The polluted horizon glows
in rusted depths of gold.

Soon, the neon lights will write
outdated messages on the canvases of night.

CRIME, OR THE LITTLE MERMAID IN THE SUBURBS

Down here in the mini-mall flatlands
it is as silent as the sea depths.

Family life buried me
in security and love, but I was made
for more than the artifices of childhood.

Trains, airplanes, any old car with
wheels will get me out of here.
I will live in the glittering cities
and embrace
the sisterhood of solitude and savagery.

I will give myself to murder and
gorged on betrayals will find a man that loathes
where I come from as much as I do.
This man, some real blood-hungry criminal,
is my savior.
I don't believe in saviors but mean to leave
this place forever anyway.

LOS ANGELES RAINING

No city is sadder when it rains.

  The thunder
those godly tremors,
     apocalyptic bombings!
  God's illegible warnings.

Let the rains come.

  Mudslides, accidents on the freeways,
the palm fronds sweep the winds, slap the rain
give themselves to the storms.
  The city streets become car washes.

The rains fall down,
  the sad rains fall.

    We have passed through the Last Days.
  Now we will wait for the light,
  the city's seasonless springtime,
its accustomed forgetting.

Let the waters come over us,
  cleansing the asphalt surfaces,
the hidden back lots.
The waters of memory visit us,

      foreign and true,
like the death we know
         the city has long ago
delivered us to.

ALIENATION

The parking lot on Main and 4th
was swarming with seagulls.
Their wings rode the smoggy air
above the parked cars.

Landing momentarily
atop neglected buildings occupied by transients,
they then resumed
obscure circling flights.

A stray seagulls
touched the sidewalk bordering
the parking lot—the populous
motherland of the homeless and sick.

What had drawn the birds to skid row?

Where did they go?
They've never been back again.

The ocean is far away.

HOLLYWOOD

Beautiful Tracy Greer
lived stately in her madness

walking the halls at Crestwood Manor
in an evening gown, a fur coat, high-heeled,

wearing diamonds and pearls
like Ginger on *Gilligan's Island*

insisting glamour was a religion
to mercilessly give oneself to

with her back to the yellow wall
statuesquely, she stood for hours,

worshiping the void.

I remember her flawless skin, her radiance
which was the same as the only star

sighting I've had in L.A.
walking home one day

on Spring Street, Cristina Ricci sat in the
passenger seat of a vintage American car,

her eyes blacked out by large
bug-like sunglasses, her glowing skin

perfect and glowing—
a star, in the prison house of the city.

THE CENTER OF THE CITY

There were blocks   you avoided
because the zombies   occupied them

I became   a witness
my innocent suburban Catholic Mexican boy eyes
        burned   as the eyes of the saints
        once burned   with visions

I saw the pilgrims   of death
prostate themselves on the sidewalks
        help and compassion   they refused
with contempt   worshiping at the altars of terror

they made you feel ashamed   inspired fear
because they had become   untouchables
        with a sort of power
the supremacy of witch doctors   and criminals

Surely, the disregard for dignity   was a perversion
        an illness   a deformity
equal to the Voodoo economics that had brought
        them   thousands upon thousands,
                to the streets

Long ago the insane asylums had closed

        But in the madhouse   of downtown
the demented kept company
                the rare believers in beauty

Gronk lived   as a sovereign
          in a kingdom-wasteland
where the law was *Devil Girl from Mars*
          and Ninón Sevilla's surreal dance numbers
from *cabaretera* movies

The alleys were sanctuaries of heroin
          where crackhead hookers   gave blow jobs
to businessmen   in Brooks Brothers suits

          The ghosts had been downtown   the longest
phantoms of shipwrecked Mexican memories
          María Félix   at the helm
the goddess who had never left
          the abandoned Million Dollar theatre

          a French playwright   a friend of a friend
remembers beautiful María Félix in 1950s Paris
          decked out in hats   jewelry and Dior
                    "like a classic courtesan"
          the courtesan ghost of Broadway
and all the dead and dying   in the streets
          were her children

And the lovers of beauty   the lost and searching
                    the dreamers
who drifted downtown   were La Doña's ghost lovers—
          second-billers, cuckolds, romantic fools

          At night   downtown was a horror movie
deprived of an audience
          screams searched for the bodies
that had housed   them
          and blood was another   splash of color
in the filthy Jackson Pollocks   of the sidewalks

PARIS

Count me among the dead,
the grand, the sorrowful,
they never deny me company.

Here, where Vallejo's grief for Spain
reached for the red banners
of a more just future,

Celan heard
the absolute syllables of the Seine
coursing beyond neon lights and human limits,

While Pizarnik, translating shadows,
seduced herself
into her homeland: madness

here, where dying begins
though the final exile is
somewhere else, in a city

that doesn't exist.

Count me among the dead,
the distant
who cannot live
anywhere else.

III The Other

IN AFRICA

I

I thought: I have been here
but I was thinking of Tijuana—
polluting traffic, hawking vendors,
tourists.

The first night I heard dogs howling
and roosters in the dark.

Accra brought back pueblos in Michoacán:
modern white houses and goats roaming the street.

For a child of the third world
the heart of darkness is the rest of the world.

II

On the beach
black boys form lines fronting the Atlantic;
they reel in nets
dragging in fish never mythologized by Christ.

A tour bus on the freeway
in the mid-day tropical heat.

Elmina's fishing port
is a postcard of exotic Africa.

The slave castle by the sea,
splendid and white, too beautiful a crime,
as elegant as a cruise ship.

A guided tour of the slave quarters
the rooms of the masters, the castle's chapel.

Centuries. Blood. Prayers. The New World.
I am so far from home.

III

Fires by shacks in the dark.

Mosquitoes and the rumors of malaria.

The Atlantic is near, its dark music in the air.

Drums in the distance.
A European man is walking by the side of the road.

Far beyond the ocean, where the slaves were taken,
is where I belong,

IV

The Spring Street sidewalk between 7th and 8th
in downtown Los Angeles at night
is consumed by lightlessness.

Crackheads under the awning
of the Mexican beauty shop
are shadows, lost or conspiring.

Sparks of a pipe, a grunt or a taunt
from the huddled obscurity,
the filthy corners of buildings.

Madness and spiritual famine.

The cry of police and ambulance sirens.

Fear—and I know I am home.

SIDONIE

after Gail Wronsky

Reading Colette
I am reminded that I, too
come from a culture steeped in taste
        variegated *nourriture:*

Banqueting, savoring what couldn't
be bought—
the metaphysics of indulgence.

Sex came with complications,
incurably guilt-sick. Love, obtuse,
        or melodramatic.

The senses, Sidonie's beloved
home, was for me darkly decorated
in Christ, the proverbial lack of money.
But look, *mole* is a lush carmine,
hefty with spices, secret excesses.
        Rancheras are operas.
The flesh, the supreme study,
        can be mastered in many languages,
all of them dead.

Longing doesn't have to cabaret itself
          in philosophy.
Sensuality can also be mute,
after all, it doesn't have much to say,
though it writes itself beautifully.
          Literature, poetry,
doesn't need Paris, chateaus,
Gallic cads or any kind of gentlemen.
It does with little commercialized California
towns entrenched by churches and canneries,
with barrio dancehalls where Mexicans
dance *cumbia* in celebration of a baptism
          or for no reason at all.

          In these mundane towns
as in the world of Colette
the spirit is manifest in what remains
of the home country, children, animals,
heartbreaks, family attachments, strawberries,
          perfumes and flowers.
Every *ranchera* houses memories
the blissful plaintiveness
          of living fully.

THE DEVIL'S MIRROR

from "The Snow Queen"

Beware of the Devil's broken mirror.
   Its arrogant scraps fly about the world,
and if they get in your eyes or heart
will make you cold, unfeeling,
    if you are not already heartless.

   Heed my advice, or you will need
the tears of the innocent. You will search
   for them in the outdated
theatres of love and the *telenovelas* of family romance,
and you will become a sadist, if you are not
    already a masochist.

Better to not come near evil mirrors,
    even in fragments,
they have dispiriting spirits
    fabricated in trollish regions,
and if they get inside of you
    will use your eyes
to make the world a reflection of hell.

WHITMAN IN THE SUBURBS

But there are some that hear him, and they know...
Edwin Arlington Robinson

I hear you
Because you are everywhere
Even in the subdivided silence.

The autumn leaves are fallen of gold
Marred with overripe seasons,
The sun's tired tarnishings.

I could almost believe you, here
Walking in the shadow of my inescapable age;
I can almost believe you
Are this light, the leaves
Piled in front yards, overrunning the driveways,
Heaped in slushy puddles,
Your soul here in the Modesto traffic, the standardized streets,
The supermarkets, thrift shops, canneries and factories,
Car washes, mini malls,
The uniform continuation of tract houses;

I could almost believe this is all you
My unease, also yours.

THE FAT GIRL

I had friend in the second grade,
a fat girl I loved through the religion
of compassionate pity and guilt
I was being given to.

She was very big, she made me sad,
and because she seemed destined
to suffer, I joined her in grief and mystery,
at night, praying and crying for her.

That's all I remember.
And that she left soon after,
that she didn't stay at
Orville Wright Elementary School.
Sometimes I recall nights
in that first house in Modesto,
the one that has been torn down,
where I cried because I knew she was leaving
and I didn't understand why God
made us different, why we had been
chosen for tragedy.

But no, it might not have been that at all.
She could have been a happy child.
But that's not what matters now.

I thought that she was taken away.
She was not Mexican or Catholic,
but we shared the Spanish language
and were alike in inexplicable ways.
I believed she was ill, and went to die
somewhere as she was supposed to.
And I have to stop my emotional mind
from making up things in conspiracy
with my unkillable Catholic heart.

I don't know who she was,
but she stayed with me,
and since then I have known her as
equivocal sorrow, my most loyal companion,
some fated friend no longer wanted.

EXILE

Stillborn nostalgias.
The city awakens to another
anonymous, sun-drenched season.

Even here, there are
those who dream of History, of
Justice, who accept being ugly
or not rich, who dream deeply,
though not always serenely.

They have not been banished.

AT THE MACDOWELL COLONY

Night after a day of snow.
Silence—winter's siesta.

Light sleeps in the snow
coating the grounds.

Walking over mushy ice
plodded by tire tracks,
my boot-heavy steps crack
cold echoes on the frost.

The wind whirls between the trees.
The dark is tinged with blue,
with the green shadows of leaves.

The porch lights of studios fall upon
sloping snow, and make it glow.

Another ten minutes
through the trudged trails,
to a warm room
that looks out onto the snow, the dark
the trees, the recessed footpaths.

RAPUNZEL

Oh, tell me, tell me,
How is it that a sorceress, a witch of sorts,
Can make a garden grow such succulent lettuce,
Organic and addictive as chocolate?

Once upon a time,
There was a hippie lady.
She must have taken too much acid
In her day, for she was wasting away
Because she couldn't get enough lettuce
From her evil neighbor's garden.

Her hippie husband was equally tripped out.
He would climb the fence to steal
The life-saving lettuce for her.
Until the sorceress caught him and he made a deal:
The lettuce for his pregnant wife's baby.
In their tripped-out world
It all made sense.

And so a child was born.
The sorceress wasn't about to forget her coupon:
The father's promise.
She showed up to redeem it,
Took the child and named it Rapunzel,
In memory of the stolen lettuce and the wife,
Who had suddenly died.

Rapunzel was a lovely child,
As healthy as a salad.
But when she turned fourteen and her virginity began to ripen,

The sorceress locked her up in a nonsensical building
Designed by a mad architect, a place without a door
Or stairs to reach her sealed prettiness up in a penthouse tower.

A few years passed, and one day one of the Kennedys
Was hiking in the sorceress' woods (she owned a whole forest,
She was a rich witch), and he heard Rapunzel singing.
The girl's loneliness and her imprisoned virginity
Gifted her a beautiful voice. The Kennedy felt her singing stir his flesh.
Although he didn't find a door to go up to his woodsy siren,
He couldn't stay away, he kept coming back
Day after day, to hear the lonely girl sing the blues to the treetops.

Then one time, he heard the sorceress
Call "Rapunzel, Rapunzel, let down your hair."
And he knew what he had to do.
He had to imitate the witch, which he did
Until dumb Rapunzel gave him away.
She blurted to her bad mother that she was heavier
Than her secret lover.
A big mistake. There's a form of vanity that's madness.
A crazy bitch boiling with incest and jealousy
Should never be told she's fat.
The sorceress took her revenge,
She had Rapunzel exiled into poverty and welfare checks,
But not before throwing the Kennedy out the window.
On the way down, the rose thorns scratched his eyes
And blinded him.

And so the Kennedy boy
Wandered blind over the country as big as his grief.
Until, years later, he came upon Rapunzel living
With five kids in a trailer in a sad Mississippi swamp town.
She was singing her old blues.
They got it on right there and then
And her tears fell on his eyes.

He could see again.
Oh, but magic can be a bag of dirty tricks.
He saw the years had made her ugly and heavy set.
In the mirrors which blindness had closed off for years
He was reacquainted with his preserved good looks.
He left Rapunzel there, as he had found her.
While in another part of the Great Country,
The sorceress' garden bloomed and she took in lovers,
Banishing the years under the plastic surgeon's knife.
Haughty and taut she walked the days of her triumph,
Untouched by the ruins of time.
Indeed, the Pinochets of the world live on and win in the end.
She felled her forest for profit and her mad architect
Built a whole city in her name.

RIMBAUD DEPARTS

The shadows I make
On Paris sidewalks
Run off without me.

Fields, barricades, burning cities,
Sunflowers, Christ,
Sperm, the incense of religion,
The night is not darkness enough.

A remote continent awaits me
Beyond erotic experiments
Mercantile martyrdoms
Bourgeois slaveries.

France, flowering with blood
And cathedrals of reason
Imprisons my senses.

I am going elsewhere
To be a violent child.

EL JALISCO

They come to pick up boys or men like themselves
At the Jalisco on Main Street,
The married men with pregnant wives waiting for them at home.
They look like the *tio* who never left the rancho:
Thick Burt Reynolds mustaches,
Tight Levi's and cowboy boots.

The ugliest drag queens parade themselves,
Sad, unconvincing amateurs who haven't
Learned to walk in their soiled Payless high heels.
But men buy them Coronas (the only drink the bar serves),
And men who could be boyfriends or pimps
Look at them with ownership.

Toward the back there are a few pool tables
And on the walls the universal icons of homosexuality:
A sultry Marilyn and the Liz of *Cat on a Hot Tin Roof.*
At the bar the immigrant men buy each other beer.
They drink half-crouched on fluffy uncomfortable seats
That dwarf them at fake wood tables.
In a nook next to the mirror facing the bar
The too-familiar image of the Virgen de Guadalupe,
Some grimy, plastic flowers at her feet.

The owners are always around,
A Mexican couple in their sixties—
He always sits glumly at the end of the bar
And his wife, wearing gold rings
On most of her fingers and a fat gold chain
Dangling a gold crucifix,
Serves beer talking *mamadas* with the guys—

They have a thirty-something daughter
Who helps at the bar
And their tall young son is the bouncer.

The hustlers come here,
The johns know where to find them.
Here is Gerardo, he has been drinking
Since the soccer game in the morning,
He's on his twentieth beer, smiling,
He lives with an old rich Argentinean couple
In the Hollywood Hills,
Takes care of their two German shepherds;
He says their Americanized Argentinean daughter,
A former model, is "*muy mala*."
She hates her parents and she hates the dogs
And she hates Gerardo.
Gerardo's smile is a boy's smile,
A happy, mischievous smile.
He's left a wife and two kids in El Salvador.
He wants to move to Las Vegas
Where he has heard there is money to be made.
At ten past one, he leaves with a gray-haired white man.

CITY RATS

Ungovernable undergrounds
our abundant kind occupy

By the rights of vileness
by the sovereignty of fear

We're rich on what the
human disposes of—
trash and transience
morsels of malaise

Populous breed

Masters of survival
we refuse to share

NIGHTS AND DEATH

after Borges

I have been many incomplete people
      searching for a final self.

I have looked into countless mirrors
to encounter the same uncanny face:
the recognizable but immeasurable
      definition of the years.

I have witnessed the moon on many nights,
the ageless moon, that remains the same
      despite my fears.

I have dreamt inside a limited number of nights,
and those dreams, in the darkened hours to come
will be the cumulative night of my death,
      my only death.

OUTSIDER ARTIST:
MARTÍN RAMÍREZ (1895-1963)

At the Dewitt State Hospital
in Auburn, California, a man is drawing
obsessive symmetrical patterns
human and animal figures
architectural fissures.

Outside is the Cold War
the nuclear age, segregation,
the advent of rock n' roll.

He is repeating diametrical traces of Mexico:
ships, rabbits, horses, *jinetes*, trumpets,
skeletal madonnas, trains, farms—
ghostly ciphers.

With nervous lines he summons
looming phantom cities,
freeways with speeding toy cars
inside truncated labyrinths.

He is charting a land
where dreams are deserts
in which unowned memories

populate
a nameless country of silence.

RAMÓN GARCÍA has published poetry in a variety of journals and anthologies including *The Americas Review*; *Best American Poetry 1996*; *Ambit* (UK); *The Floating Borderlands: Twenty-Five Years of U.S.-Hispanic Literature*; *Margie: The American Journal of Poetry*; *Crab Orchard Review*; *Poetry Salzburg Review* (Austria); *Borderlands: The Texas Poetry Review*; *Los Angeles Review*, and *Mandorla: New Writing from the Americas*. He is Associate Professor in Chicana/o Studies at California State University, Northridge.

Breinigsville, PA USA
05 October 2010
246681BV00002B/4/P